LES PETITS PLATS
FRANÇAIS
SIMON & SCHUSTER
ILLUSTRATED

divine chocolate desserts

JOSÉ MARÉCHAL

Photography by Akiko Ida

SIMON &
SCHUSTER

London · New York · Sydney · Toronto

A CBS COMPANY

English language edition published in Great Britain by
Simon and Schuster UK Ltd, 2010
A CBS Company

Copyright © Marabout 2010

SIMON AND SCHUSTER ILLUSTRATED BOOKS
Simon & Schuster UK
222 Gray's Inn Road
London WC1X 8HB
www.simonandschuster.co.uk

1 2 3 4 5 6 7 8 9 10

Translation: Prudence Ivey
Copy editor English language: Nicki Lampon

Colour reproduction by Dot Gradations Ltd, UK
Printed and bound in U.A.E.

ISBN 978-0-85720-110-2

Contents

Equipment

Piping bags and glasses

Much more practical than teaspoons or mini ladles, piping bags are an indispensable tool for the assembly of these layered desserts. You can find disposable ones at the supermarket or reusable ones in specialist cook shops. You can also use a freezer bag with one corner cut off.

Use plain, round glasses or, if you don't have any, any small glass will do just as well.

Chantilly cream (whipped cream)

This is the base for all your chocolate desserts in some form or other – vanilla, chocolate, spiced or fruity.

For a successful Chantilly cream, use either whipping or double cream. It must have a fat content of 33% or more. The mixing bowl and the cream should be very cold.

Paper cone

For more delicate chocolate decorations, filaments, small drawings, writing, etc.

Cut a long-edged triangle of greaseproof paper, roll it and tuck the long edges in (see photographs opposite) and you have a mini piping bag for ultra precision.

Siphon...

...for your Chantilly cream? Yes but not exclusively! A siphon will transform fruit juice, coulis or coconut milk into a light mousse in the blink of an eye.

Chocolate crumble

Preparation time: 30 minutes +
1½ hours chilling
Cooking time: 20 minutes
Makes 6–8 desserts

150 ml (5¼ fl oz) chocolate icing
(see recipe on page 34)
2 dessertspoons cocoa powder

Chocolate crumble
100 g (3½ oz) plain flour
100 g (3½ oz) icing sugar
30 g (1 oz) cocoa powder
70 g (2½ oz) ground almonds
125 g (4½ oz) butter, softened

Chocolate cream
200 ml (7 fl oz) milk
300 ml (10½ fl oz) whipping cream
6 egg yolks
70 g (2½ oz) icing sugar
250 g (8¾ oz) dark chocolate
(minimum 58% cocoa solids),
broken into small pieces

Put all the crumble ingredients in a mixing bowl. Mix with your fingers until they reach a breadcrumb consistency. Leave to cool in the fridge for at least 20 minutes.

For the chocolate cream, heat the milk and the cream in a saucepan over a medium heat. Beat the egg yolks and the sugar together vigorously then pour the boiling cream into the beaten eggs. Mix well then return the pan to a low heat. The cream will gradually thicken and cover the back of a spoon but it must not boil. Pour the hot custard over the dark chocolate pieces and mix together well.

Fill your serving glasses two-thirds full with the custard and place in the fridge for at least an hour.

Preheat the oven to 180°C (fan oven 160°C), Gas Mark 4.

Scatter the crumble on to a baking sheet and cook for around 8 minutes. Leave to cool for 15 minutes.

Meanwhile, top the desserts with the chocolate icing and return to the fridge.

Just before serving, sprinkle the crumble over the top and then finish with a dusting of cocoa powder.

Chocolate delight

Preparation time: 45 minutes +
  2 hours chilling
Cooking time: 18–20 minutes
Makes 8–10 desserts

coco pops

Milk chocolate ganache
150 ml (5¼ fl oz) milk
100 ml (3½ fl oz) whipping cream
250 g (8¾ oz) milk chocolate,
  broken into small pieces

White chocolate mousse
1 sheet of gelatine
250 ml (8¾ fl oz) whipping cream
150 g (5¼ oz) white chocolate,
  broken into small pieces

Dark chocolate mousse
250 ml (8¾ fl oz) milk
3 egg yolks
30 g (1 oz) icing sugar
200 g (7 oz) dark chocolate
  (minimum 70% cocoa solids),
  broken into small pieces
150 ml (5¼ oz) whipping cream

To make the milk chocolate ganache, bring the milk and cream to the boil over a medium heat. Place the chocolate in a bowl, pour over the boiling mixture and mix well until you have a smooth ganache. Fill your serving glasses a quarter full and put in the fridge.

For the white chocolate mousse, soften the gelatine in cold water. Bring half the cream to the boil in a saucepan over a low heat then add the gelatine and melt. Place the white chocolate in a bowl and pour over the hot cream. Mix well then leave to cool at room temperature.

Whip the remaining cream until firm, then gently fold into the white chocolate cream.

Generously sprinkle the ganache with the coco pops then add a layer of white chocolate mousse. Return to the fridge.

For the dark chocolate mousse, heat the milk in a saucepan over a medium heat. Vigorously beat the egg yolks and the sugar together in a mixing bowl then pour over the boiling milk. Mix well and return to a low heat. The mixture will thicken and begin to stick to the spoon but it must not boil. Pour over the dark chocolate and mix well. Leave to cool at room temperature for a few minutes.

Whip the cream then gently fold in the dark chocolate cream.

Pour into the glasses in a final layer then return to the fridge for at least 1 hour.

Tip: Decorate the desserts as you like; add black cherries, chocolate icing, coco pops, chocolate shavings or chips just before serving.

Milk chocolate cream pots with lemon thyme

Preparation time: 20 minutes +
  2 hours chilling
Cooking time: 60–90 minutes
Makes 8–12 desserts

120 ml (4¼ fl oz) milk
400 ml (14 fl oz) whipping cream
4 sprigs of lemon thyme
125 g (4½ oz) milk chocolate,
  broken into small pieces
3 egg yolks
60 g (2 oz) icing sugar

Heat the milk and cream over a medium heat. As soon as they start bubbling, remove from the heat, add 3 sprigs of thyme, and leave to infuse for 2–3 minutes.

Place the milk chocolate in a bowl and strain the mixture over. Mix well.

In another bowl, vigorously beat the egg yolks and the sugar together. Pour over the chocolate cream and mix well.

Preheat the oven to 90°C (fan oven 70°C).

Divide the mixture between your serving glasses and place in a roasting tin. Add water to the tin, making sure it does not come above the tops of the glasses. Cook in the oven for 60–90 minutes, depending on the size of the glasses. Make sure the temperature of the oven does not exceed 100°C (fan oven 80°C).

As soon as the desserts are cooked, put them in the fridge for at least 2 hours.

Before serving, decorate the desserts with the remaining sprig of thyme, divided between the glasses.

Mikado cage

Preparation time: 40–50 minutes
+ 1 hour chilling
Makes 6–8 desserts

500 g (1 lb 1½ oz) chocolate cream
(see recipe on page 6)
around 80 Mikado chocolate
biscuits
12 chocolate bears (or any animal-
shaped chocolate)
40 g (1½ oz) marzipan (optional)
yellow and brown food colouring
(optional)

Banana mousse
4 sheets of gelatine
3 bananas
juice of 2 lemons
100 g (3½ oz) icing sugar
50 ml (1¾ fl oz) dark rum
200 ml (7 fl oz) whipping cream
1 teaspoon vanilla extract or ½ a
vanilla pod
3 egg whites

For the banana mousse, first soften
the gelatine in cold water.

Peel the bananas and mix with the
lemon juice and half the sugar until
you have a fine purée. Gently heat
the rum and add the gelatine, then
mix with the banana purée.

Whip the cream, add the vanilla then
carefully fold in the banana purée.

Whisk the egg whites to snowy
peaks, add the remaining sugar
and whisk again for 1–2 minutes.
Carefully fold into the banana
mousse.

Refrigerate for at least 1 hour.

Pour a bed of chocolate cream into
the bottom of your serving glasses
and put in the fridge. (You could do
this step before preparing the banana
mousse, saving yourself some time at
the end.)

Once the chocolate cream is cool
and firm, plant the Mikado biscuits in
the glasses, near the edge, around
1 cm (½ inch) apart.

Fill a piping bag with banana mousse
and fill the glasses two-thirds full.

Finally, put your chocolate animal in
its cage and make some little
marzipan bananas, colouring them
with the food colouring, if you wish to
really impress your guests.

Melting chocolate bites

Preparation time: 15 minutes the day before + 35 minutes + 3 hours chilling
Makes 15–18 bites

You will need an ice cube tray or silicone mould and 15–18 wooden sticks

oil for deep frying

Chocolate ganache
150 ml (5¼ fl oz) whipping cream
250 g (8¾ oz) dark chocolate, broken into small pieces
50 g (1¾ oz) butter, cut into small cubes
3 drops of coffee extract

Batter
175 g (6¼ oz) flour
175 g (6¼ oz) potato starch
1 egg
1 egg white
a little cold water

The day before, prepare the ganache. In a saucepan, bring the cream to the boil over a low heat. Pour into a mixing bowl over the broken chocolate, add the butter and mix well until you have a smooth ganache. Add the coffee extract.

With a spoon, divide the ganache between the ice cube trays or silicone moulds and put in the freezer.

As soon as the ganache is very firm, plant a stick in the centre of each cube then return to the freezer.

For the batter, mix the flour, starch, egg and egg white in a bowl until you have a smooth paste that is quite thick. Add a little cold water to loosen it slightly (it should be runny but not too much, just enough to cover the chocolate cubes). Put in the fridge.

Heat the oil over a medium heat.

Turn out the chocolate cubes, roll them lightly in your hands to form them into balls and return to the freezer.

Whisk the batter and, once the oil is hot, dip the bites, one by one, in the batter. Drop them in the oil for 1–2 minutes to colour the batter and melt the ganache.

Serve immediately.

Crunchy chocolate with two chocolate mousses

Preparation time: 35 minutes +
1 hour 30 minutes chilling
Cooking time: 10 minutes
Makes 8–12 desserts

Dark and white chocolate mousses
500 ml (17½ fl oz) milk
6 egg yolks
20 g (¾ oz) icing sugar
200 g (7 oz) dark chocolate
(minimum 55% cocoa solids),
broken into small pieces
250 g (8¾ oz) white chocolate,
broken into small pieces
300 ml (10½ fl oz) whipping cream

Crunchy chocolate
400 g (14 oz) dark, white or milk
chocolate
2 dessertspoons oil
250 g (8¾ oz) coco pops + 125 g
(4½ oz) for decoration

To make the mousses, heat the milk in a saucepan over a medium heat. Vigorously beat the egg yolks and sugar together then pour the boiling milk over them. Mix well and return to a low heat. The mix will thicken gently and cover the back of a spoon but it must not boil.

Pour half the milky custard into a bowl containing the dark chocolate, and the other half into a bowl containing the white chocolate. Mix both well. Leave to cool at room temperature.

Whip the cream then divide between the two bowls of chocolate, folding in gently. Put in the fridge for at least an hour.

For the crunchy chocolate, melt the chocolate with the oil in the microwave or in a bowl over a pan of simmering water. Add the coco pops. Place a sheet of greaseproof paper on the work surface and pour the chocolate on to it. Smooth gently with a spatula. Cover with another piece of greaseproof paper and roll lightly with a rolling pin until you have a fine smooth sheet of crunchy chocolate. Put in the fridge.

Gently stir each well-chilled mousse to loosen them slightly and fill two piping bags.

Break the crunchy chocolate into long irregular pieces that will fit inside your serving glasses.

Fill the glasses one by one: with one hand, hold the piece of crunchy chocolate in the middle of the glass and, with the other hand, pipe in the mousses, one on either side. Tap the bottom of each glass gently on the work surface so that the mousse fits the shape of the glass.

Return to the fridge for at least 30 minutes and sprinkle with coco pops before serving.

Milk chocolate mousse with caramel

Preparation time: 30 minutes +
1 hour chilling
Cooking time: 15–20 minutes
Makes 6–8 desserts

30 sponge fingers

Mousse
100 ml (3½ fl oz) milk
4 eggs, separated
120 g (4¼ oz) icing sugar
250 g (8¾ oz) milk chocolate,
  broken into pieces

Caramel
200 g (7 oz) icing sugar
150 ml (5¼ fl oz) water
½ vanilla pod
50 ml (1¾ fl oz) olive oil

To make the mousse, bring the milk to the boil over a low heat. Beat the egg yolks and half the sugar together in a mixing bowl, then pour in the boiling milk and mix well. Return to a low heat and leave to gently thicken and cover the back of a spoon (do not allow to boil).

Pour the hot cream over the milk chocolate and mix well. Leave to cool at room temperature for around 30 minutes.

Whisk the egg whites until they form stiff peaks and then add the rest of the sugar, continuing to beat for 2–3 minutes to make a meringue. Fold one-third of the egg whites into the chocolate cream to loosen, then gently fold in the rest.

Crush the sponge fingers until they become powdered, then fill the bottom of your serving glasses with a 1 cm (½ inch) layer of this powder. With a piping bag or a spoon, add a layer of chocolate mousse. Repeat once more, leaving around 1 cm (½ inch) at the top of each glass.

Put in the fridge for at least an hour.

For the caramel, heat the sugar and a third of the water in a saucepan over a medium heat. Once it is a golden caramel colour, remove from the heat, rest the saucepan in the sink and, holding it at arm's length, pour in the rest of the water (watch out for burns and scalds, it will steam).

Return the saucepan to the heat for a few seconds, stirring to thin the caramel.

With a small knife, scrape the seeds from the vanilla pod into the caramel then add the olive oil.

Just before serving, blend the caramel and oil together with an electric whisk or blender. Pour on to the top of the mousses.

Tip: The liquid caramel will keep very well in the fridge or at room temperature.

Pépito coffee desserts

Preparation time 20 minutes +
  1 hour chilling
Makes 4–6 desserts

You will need glasses the same
  diameter as your biscuits

48 chocolate covered shortbread
  biscuits (Pépito biscuits)
500 ml (17½ fl oz) cold coffee

Coffee cream
6 egg yolks
100 g (3½ oz) icing sugar
400 g (14 oz) mascarpone
50 ml (1¾ fl oz) coffee extract

To make the coffee cream, beat the egg yolks and the sugar together until you have a smooth, mousse-like mixture. Gradually add the mascarpone and the coffee extract and mix vigorously.

Lightly soak the biscuits in the cold coffee and put two biscuits at the bottom of each glass.

Fill a piping bag with the coffee cream and add a layer on top of the biscuits.

Continue to alternate biscuits and cream, finishing with a biscuit layer.

Cover the glasses with clingfilm and put in the fridge for at least an hour.

Tip: Pépito biscuits are a chocolate covered shortbread popular in France, they are available online. Alternatively use any chocolate covered shortbread biscuit as an substitute.

Cherry-topped pots

Preparation time: 15 minutes the day before + 20 minutes + 1 hour chilling the day before + 1 hour chilling

Cooking time: 1 hour 20 minutes the day before + 8 minutes

Makes 8–12 desserts

200 g (7 oz) frozen cherries
12 cherries covered in chocolate

Cherry custard
100 ml (3½ fl oz) whole milk
6 egg yolks
75 g (2½ oz) icing sugar
500 ml (17½ fl oz) whipping cream

Chocolate and cherry ganache
200 ml (7 fl oz) milk
100 ml (3½ fl oz) whipping cream
150 g (5¼ oz) dark chocolate (minimum 55% cocoa solids), broken into pieces
125 g (4½ oz) milk chocolate, broken into pieces
50 ml (1¾ fl oz) cherry liqueur

Cherry cream
500 ml (17½ fl oz) whipping cream
2–3 dessertspoons cherry jam

The day before, prepare the cherry custard. Heat the milk over a medium heat. In a bowl, vigorously beat the egg yolks and the sugar together then add the cold cream. Pour in the boiling milk and mix well. Leave in the fridge for at least 1 hour.

Preheat the oven to 90°C (fan oven 70°C).

Add 2–3 cm (¾–1¼ inches) of custard and a few frozen cherries to each serving glass and place in a roasting tin. Add enough water to come halfway up the sides of the glasses and cook for around 1 hour 15 minutes. Make sure the temperature does not exceed 100°C (fan oven 80°C). Once cooked, put the glasses in the fridge.

The next day, make the ganache. Heat the milk and cream over a low heat until they boil. Place both chocolates in a mixing bowl and pour over the milk and cream mixture. Mix well to melt the chocolate then add the liqueur. Add a layer of ganache, around 1 cm (½ inch) thick, to the glasses. Return to the fridge for 1 hour.

For the cherry cream, whip the cream then gently fold in the jam. With a piping bag, fill the glasses with cream.

Decorate with the chocolate-covered cherries.

Black forest gâteau

Preparation time: 20 minutes +
  30 minutes chilling
Makes 8–12 desserts

800 g (1 lb 12 oz) chocolate cake or
  chocolate brownies
200 ml (7 fl oz) cherry syrup or
  liqueur
50 ml (1¾ fl oz) water
500 g (1 lb 1½ oz) stoned cherries
250 g (8¾ oz) chocolate shavings

Vanilla cream
500 ml (17½ fl oz) very cold
  whipping cream
100 g (3½ oz) icing sugar
½ vanilla pod or a few drops of
  vanilla extract

To make the vanilla cream, pour the whipping cream into a food mixer or a very cold mixing bowl. If it is not cold enough, place in another larger bowl filled with ice. Whip the cream, then add the sugar and seeds from the vanilla pod or vanilla extract. Whip again to mix. Leave in the fridge for no more than a few hours.

Cut the chocolate cake or brownies into pieces and put a layer into the bottom of each serving glass, pressing down gently with your fingertips. Dilute the cherry syrup or liqueur with the water and pour a little over the cake. Add a few cherries. Add a layer of cream then repeat the steps with another layer of cake, etc. until the glasses are full. Put in the fridge for around 30 minutes before decorating with chocolate shavings and serving.

White chocolate desserts with strawberries and wasabi

Preparation time: 30 minutes +
1 hour chilling
Cooking time: 10 minutes
Makes 6–8 desserts

White chocolate mousse
2 sheets of gelatine
500 ml (17½ fl oz) whipping cream
300 g (10½ oz) white chocolate,
broken into pieces

**White chocolate and wasabi
ganache**
150 ml (17½ fl oz) whipping cream
15 g (½ oz) powdered wasabi
140 g (5 oz) white chocolate, broken
into pieces

Strawberry purée
400 g (14 oz) strawberries, washed
and hulled
40 g (1½ oz) icing sugar
juice of half a lemon
2 dessertspoons water

For the white chocolate mousse, first soften the gelatine in cold water. In a saucepan, bring 200 ml (7 fl oz) of the cream to the boil over a low heat, melt the gelatine in it then pour over the white chocolate in a bowl. Mix well to melt the chocolate and leave to cool for 8–10 minutes at room temperature.

Whip the rest of the cream then gently fold into the white chocolate mixture.

Fill your serving glasses a third full with the mousse then leave in the fridge for at least 40 minutes.

To make the ganache, mix the cream and the wasabi in a saucepan over a low heat and bring to the boil. Pour into a mixing bowl over the chocolate and mix well until you have a smooth ganache. Add a fine layer of ganache to the glasses and return them to the fridge for at least 20 minutes.

Cut the strawberries into small pieces. Lightly crush them with a fork in a small bowl with the icing sugar, lemon juice and water until you have a slightly liquid purée.

Just before serving, add a layer of strawberry purée to the glasses.

Milk chocolate and raspberry mousses

Preparation time: 30 minutes +
1 hour 15 minutes chilling
Cooking time: 6 minutes
Makes 8–12 desserts

100 ml (3½ fl oz) raspberry syrup
100 ml (3½ fl oz) water
36 Roses de Reims biscuits (see
  Tip)
fresh raspberries, chocolate pieces
  and/or a little raspberry coulis, to
  decorate

**Milk chocolate and raspberry
  mousse**
150 ml (5¼ fl oz) milk
400 ml (14 fl oz) whipping cream
350 g (12¼ oz) milk chocolate,
  broken into pieces
100 g (3½ oz) raspberries

To make the mousse, bring the milk
and 100 ml (3½ fl oz) of cream to the
boil over a medium heat. Place the
chocolate in a bowl and pour over the
boiling mixture. Mix well, then add
the raspberries, beating until smooth.
Leave to cool at room temperature for
around 15 minutes.

Whip the remaining cold cream then
gently fold into the chocolate mixture.

In a bowl, mix the raspberry syrup
and water together. Crumble the
biscuits into the syrup one by one,
then add a layer of this mixture to the
bottom of each serving glass. With a
piping bag or a spoon, add the
chocolate and raspberry mousse.

Add more layers depending on the
size of the glasses and the desired
effect. Leave in the fridge for at least
30 minutes between each step.

Decorate with fresh raspberries,
chocolate and/or a little raspberry
coulis to personalise your desserts.

Tip: Biscuits Roses de Reims are
sweet, pink-coloured biscuits from
the Reims region of France. They are
available online.

Morello cherry, coconut and white chocolate layers

Preparation time: 20 minutes +
40 minutes chilling for the first
layer + 30 minutes chilling for
the others
Cooking time: 7 minutes
Makes 4–6 desserts

150 g (5¼ oz) morello cherries
50 g (1¾ oz) grated coconut, lightly
toasted

**Coconut and white chocolate
cream**
2 sheets of gelatine
400 ml (14 fl oz) coconut milk
150 g (5¼ oz) white chocolate,
broken into pieces
100 g (3½ oz) grated coconut

To make the cream, first soften the gelatine in cold water. Heat the coconut milk to boiling then melt the gelatine in it. Place the chocolate and grated coconut in a bowl, pour over the coconut milk and mix well. Set aside to cool at room temperature.

Pour 1–2 cm (½–¾ inch) of the cream into your serving glasses then leave to cool in the fridge for around 40 minutes.

Add a layer of morello cherries and a little of their syrup then cover with another layer of cream. Return to the fridge and continue in this way until the glasses are full.

Just before serving, decorate the glasses with the toasted coconut.

Black and red

Preparation time: 30 minutes + at
least 2 hours chilling
Cooking time: 20 minutes
Makes 6–8 desserts

Red
250 g (8¾ oz) strawberries, washed
    and hulled
100 g (3½ oz) redcurrants
150 g (5¼ oz) raspberries
3 sheets of gelatine
200 ml (7 fl oz) raspberry coulis

Black
250 ml (8¾ fl oz) chocolate icing
    (see recipe on page 34)
300 ml (3½ fl oz) milk
300 ml (3½ fl oz) whipping cream
7 egg yolks
80 g (2¾ oz) icing sugar
300 g (10½ oz) dark chocolate
    (minimum 55% cocoa solids),
    broken into pieces

For the red half, cut the strawberries
into small pieces and mix with the
redcurrants and raspberries.

Soften the gelatine in cold water.
In a small saucepan, gently heat the
raspberry coulis then remove from
the heat and dissolve the gelatine in
it. Pour over the fruit and mix gently.

Half fill the glasses with a spoon then
put in the fridge for 30–40 minutes.

For the black half, gently warm the
chocolate icing. Pour a little over the
jellied fruit then return the glasses to
the fridge.

Heat the milk and the cream over a
medium heat.

Whisk the egg yolks and the sugar
together then pour the boiling cream
mixture over them. Mix well and
return to the heat. The cream will
gently thicken and cover the back
of the spoon, but it must not boil.

Place the chocolate in a bowl, pour
the hot cream over and mix well.

Fill the glasses and return to the
fridge for 1 hour 30 minutes.

Tips: To achieve the diagonal effect
seen in the photograph, lean the
glasses against a mound of flour in
a bowl before putting them in the
fridge.

You can decorate the desserts with
a little red-coloured crumble as in the
photograph.

Apricot, ginger and chocolate desserts

Preparation time: 40 minutes +
30 minutes chilling
Cooking time: 30 minutes
Makes 8–12 desserts

250 g (8¾ oz) ginger biscuits

Chocolate icing
150 ml (5¼ fl oz) water
180 g (6¼ oz) icing sugar
4 sheets of gelatine
60 g (2 oz) cocoa powder
100 ml (3½ fl oz) whipping cream

Apricot jam
500 ml (17½ fl oz) water
125 g (4½ oz) icing sugar
500 g (17½ oz) dried apricots
30 g (1 oz) crystallised ginger

To make the icing, heat the water and the sugar in a saucepan until the water boils. Soften the gelatine in cold water. Add the cocoa powder to the boiling syrup, keeping it over a low heat and stirring constantly for 5 minutes. In another saucepan, heat the cream until it boils, then pour into the chocolate syrup. Mix well over a low heat for 5 more minutes then take off the heat. Leave to cool for 15–20 minutes then dissolve the gelatine in the mixture. Leave to cool.

For the apricot jam, heat the water and sugar until the water boils, then add the apricots for 5–7 minutes. Remove the apricots from the syrup and mix them with 3 dessertspoons of syrup and the crystallised ginger until you have a jam-like consistency.

Grind the biscuits into a fine powder.

With a spoon or piping bag, fill the glasses a third full with apricot jam then sprinkle with the crushed biscuit. Lightly warm the icing then add a layer so that the glasses are two-thirds full. Leave in the fridge for at least 30 minutes so the icing thickens slightly.

Before serving, decorate the glasses with the rest of the crushed biscuits and apricot jam.

Bananas with chocolate and caramelised peanuts

Preparation time: 30 minutes +
1 hour 30 minutes chilling
Cooking time: 15 minutes
Makes 6–8 desserts

100 g (3½ oz) icing sugar
4 bananas, thickly sliced
125 g (4½ oz) caramelised peanuts

Double chocolate cream
200 ml (7 fl oz) milk
150 ml (5¼ fl oz) whipping cream
1 dessertspoon thick double cream
50 g (1¾ oz) milk chocolate, broken
  into small pieces
150 g (5¼ oz) dark chocolate
  (minimum 58% cocoa solids),
  broken into small pieces
3 egg yolks

Put 50 g (1¾ oz) of sugar in a pan, heat over a medium heat and, once it starts to caramelise, add half the bananas, colouring them for 30 seconds on each side. Repeat with the remaining sugar and bananas.

For the double chocolate cream, heat the milk and both creams on a medium heat until they boil. Place both chocolates in a bowl, pour over the boiling cream mixture and mix well until you have a smooth paste. Add the egg yolks and mix again.

Carefully cover the bottom of your serving glasses with the caramelised banana pieces.

Pour a layer of chocolate cream over the bananas.

Leave in the fridge for at least 1 hour 30 minutes to set the cream.

With a rolling pin, crush the peanuts into large chunks and sprinkle over the desserts just before serving.

White chocolate and citrus layers

Preparation time: 30 minutes +
  1 hour chilling
Cooking time: 5 minutes
Makes 6–8 desserts

7 oranges
6 grapefruits
5 limes
24 sponge fingers
800 g (1 lb 12 oz) white chocolate
  mousse (see recipe on page 26)
3 sheets of gelatine

With a small knife, peel the fruit and segment it, removing the membranes but keeping as much juice as possible. Put in separate bowls.

Cut the fruit segments into small pieces and leave in their juices.

Crumble the sponge fingers and place a layer of them at the bottom of each glass, then cover with the orange juice and flesh.

Add a layer of chocolate mousse around 2 cm (¾ inch) thick and put in the fridge to thicken the mousse.

Soften the gelatine in cold water. Gently heat the grapefruit juice and melt the gelatine in it, then add the grapefruit flesh. Set aside.

Add another layer of sponge fingers to the glasses then add the lime juice and flesh and a final layer of chocolate mousse.

Add a layer of grapefruit jelly and put in the fridge for at least 20 minutes before serving.

Pear, passion fruit and chocolate desserts

Preparation time: 45 minutes +
45 minutes chilling
Cooking time: 30 minutes
Makes 8–12 desserts

75 g (2½ oz) demerara sugar
(optional)

Pear jam
15 pears, poached
70 g (2½ oz) icing sugar
3 scoops of passion fruit sorbet
seeds from 4 passion fruit

Chocolate cream
4 sheets of gelatine
500 ml (17½ fl oz) milk
200 ml (7 fl oz) whipping cream
8 egg yolks
200 g (7 oz) icing sugar
40 g (1½ oz) cornflour
30 g (1 oz) cocoa powder
4 egg whites

To make the pear jam, cut off and
reserve the tops from 8–12 of the
poached pears (depending on how
many serving glasses you have).
Cut all the rest of the pear into large
chunks. Heat the sugar in a pan until
lightly caramelised then add the
cubed pear and cook over a medium
heat for 5–6 minutes. Add the sorbet
and passion fruit seeds and cook for
6–8 minutes, stirring constantly.
Leave to cool.

For the chocolate cream, soften the
gelatine in cold water. In a pan, bring
the milk and the cream to the boil.

Meanwhile, vigorously beat the egg
yolks and 80 g (2¾ oz) of the sugar
together then add the cornflour and
cocoa powder. Pour in the boiling milk
and cream and mix well then return
to a low heat, stirring constantly for
5–7 minutes. Pour the cream into a
new bowl to stop the cooking then
add the gelatine.

Whisk the egg whites to stiff
peaks, adding the remaining icing
sugar at the end and beating to get
a meringue mix. Gently fold into the
warm chocolate cream.

With a spoon, share the pear jam
between the glasses. Using a piping
bag, fill the glasses with chocolate
cream then add the pear tops. Add
a little more chocolate cream around
the edges. Leave in the fridge for at
least 45 minutes.

If you wish, sprinkle with demerara
sugar before serving and lightly
caramelise with a blow torch.

Chocolate with green tea

Preparation time: 30 minutes +
1 hour 30 minutes chilling
Cooking time: 15 minutes
Makes 6–8 desserts

You will need a 500 ml (17½ fl oz)
siphon with gas cylinder

24 sponge fingers, cut into small
pieces

Chocolate cream
400 ml (14 fl oz) milk
600 ml (21 fl oz) whipping cream
12 egg yolks
130 g (4½ oz) icing sugar
500 g (1 lb 1½ oz) dark chocolate
(minimum 50–55% cocoa solids),
broken into small pieces

Green tea syrup
1 litre (1¾ pints) mineral water
140 g (5 oz) icing sugar
30 g (1 oz) powdered green tea
4 sheets of gelatine

For the chocolate cream, heat the milk and cream over a medium heat. Beat the egg yolks and sugar together vigorously then pour in the boiling cream. Mix well and return to a low heat. The cream will lightly thicken and cover the back of the spoon but must not boil. Place the chocolate in a bowl, pour the hot cream over and mix well. Keep at room temperature.

For the green tea syrup, heat the water and sugar until boiling. Remove from the heat then add the green tea powder.

Soften the gelatine in cold water. Dissolve in a quarter of the green tea syrup. Keep at room temperature.

Add a layer of biscuits to each serving glass. Pour in some of the green tea syrup (without gelatine) and press down with your fingertips.

Add a layer of chocolate cream then place the desserts in the fridge for around 30 minutes.

Repeat with a second layer of biscuit, tea and chocolate cream then return to the fridge for 30 more minutes.

Once the desserts are set, add 1 cm (½ inch) of green tea syrup with gelatine and return to the fridge.

Just before serving, take the remaining syrup and siphon into the glasses to decorate your desserts.

Mint chocolate desserts

Preparation time: 50 minutes
Cooking time: 10 minutes
Makes 8–12 desserts

Mint chocolate cream
150 ml (5¼ fl oz) milk
150 g (5¼ oz) dark chocolate
   (minimum 70% cocoa solids),
   broken into small pieces
2 egg yolks
20 ml (¾ fl oz) mint liqueur or syrup
150 ml (5¼ fl oz) whipping cream

Mint and white chocolate icing
50 ml (1¾ fl oz) whipping cream
20 ml (¾ fl oz) mint liqueur or syrup
125 g (4½ oz) white chocolate,
   broken into small pieces

Decoration
200 g (7 oz) dark chocolate, broken
   into small pieces
1 dessertspoon oil
125 g (4½ oz) chocolate dragées or
   chocolate-covered beans
150 ml (5¼ fl oz) mint syrup or
   liqueur
8–12 mint leaves

For the mint chocolate cream, heat the milk over a medium heat until it boils. Pour over the chocolate in a bowl. Mix well until smooth then add the egg yolks and mint liqueur. Leave to cool for a few minutes.

Meanwhile, whip the cream then fold in the chocolate mint mixture. Keep in the fridge.

For the icing, heat the cream and mint liqueur over a medium heat or in the microwave. Pour over the white chocolate in a bowl. Mix and keep at room temperature.

Melt the dark chocolate and oil in the microwave or in a bowl over a pan of simmering water.

Meanwhile, put a few chocolate dragées or beans in the bottom of each glass then pour in the mint liqueur until they are covered.

Fill a paper cone (see page 4 for instructions on how to make one) with the melted dark chocolate, or use a small spoon, and pipe over a thin layer of chocolate on top of the mint liqueur.

Put in the fridge for a few minutes to set the chocolate.

Gently stir the mint chocolate cream to loosen it a little then put it in a piping bag.

Add a layer of the cream to the desserts, leaving ½ cm (¼ inch) at the top, then return to the fridge.

With a small paintbrush, cover the mint leaves on each side with a layer of melted chocolate. Place them carefully on a plate covered with cling film and leave them to harden in the fridge.

Lightly warm the icing and fill the glasses with it. Put in the fridge.

Just before serving, decorate each glass with a chocolate-covered mint leaf.

Lemon and chocolate delights

Preparation time. 20 minutes +
1 hour 30 minutes chilling
Cooking time: 10 minutes
Makes 8–10 desserts

175 g (6¼ oz) dark chocolate,
broken into pieces
a few drops of oil

**White chocolate and lemon
mousse**
200 ml (7 fl oz) lemon juice
6 egg yolks
3 whole eggs
80 g (2¾ oz) icing sugar
90 g (3¼ oz) unsalted butter
150 g (5¼ oz) white chocolate,
broken into pieces
200 ml (7 fl oz) whipping cream

For the white chocolate and lemon mousse, gently heat the lemon juice in a saucepan. Meanwhile, beat the egg yolks, whole eggs and sugar in a mixing bowl then pour in the hot lemon juice.

Return the mix to a low heat and cook until it thickens, stirring constantly to ensure that it doesn't burn. Away from the heat add the butter and white chocolate, mix well then keep in the fridge.

Whip the cream. Once the white chocolate and lemon cream is really cold, carefully fold in the whipped cream with a spatula.

Melt the dark chocolate with the oil in a microwave or in a bowl over a pan of simmering water.

Meanwhile, fill a piping bag with the white chocolate and lemon mousse and add an initial layer in the bottom of each serving glass.

Fill a paper cone (see page 4 for instructions on how to make one) with the melted dark chocolate. Use the cone, or a teaspoon, to draw some fine lines of chocolate over the top of the mousse and against the edge of the glass.

Add a second layer of mousse and then chocolate and continue until you reach the top of the glass.

Put in the fridge and serve well chilled.

Spiced oranges with hot chocolate gingerbread

Preparation time: 20 minutes
Cooking time: 12 minutes
Makes 4–6 desserts

You will need 4–6 small lollipop
  sticks

Spiced oranges
4–6 oranges
300 ml (10½ fl oz) orange juice
1 dessertspoon icing sugar
1 teaspoon cinnamon
1 teaspoon ground ginger

Hot chocolate
300 ml (10½ fl oz) milk
100 ml (3½ fl oz) whipping cream
70 g (2½ oz) dark chocolate, broken
  into pieces
70 g (2½ oz) gingerbread

With a small knife, peel the oranges
then cut them in regular slices.

Reassemble the oranges and secure
each with a lollipop stick. Keep in the
fridge.

In a saucepan, and over a medium
heat, heat the orange juice, sugar and
spices until boiling then leave to cool.

Put all the hot chocolate ingredients
in a saucepan and heat very gently,
stirring with a whisk until the
chocolate and the gingerbread are
melted and the mixture is warm.

Put each orange in a glass and pour
over the spiced juice.

Serve the hot chocolate separately
or pour directly over the oranges just
before serving.

Crunchy chocolate orange desserts

Preparation time. 30 minutes +
40 minutes chilling
Cooking time: 12 minutes
Makes 8–12 desserts

Chocolate orange cream

200 ml (7 fl oz) whipping cream
80 ml (2¾ fl oz) orange juice
50 g (1¾ oz) butter
80 g (2¾ oz) dark chocolate
 (minimum 70% cocoa solids),
 broken into pieces
150 g (5¼ oz) milk chocolate,
 broken into pieces
20 ml (¾ fl oz) orange liqueur

Crunchy chocolate

250 g (8¾ oz) dark chocolate,
 broken into pieces
200 g (7 oz) cigarettes russes or
 crêpes dentelles
50 g (1¾ oz) crystallised orange or
 chocolate-covered candied peel +
 50 g (1¾ oz) for decoration

To make the chocolate orange cream, heat the whipping cream, orange juice and butter in a saucepan until the mixture starts to simmer. Place both chocolates in a bowl and pour over the cream mixture. Mix well with a whisk until you have a smooth cream. Add the orange liqueur. Keep in the fridge.

For the crunchy chocolate, melt the chocolate in the microwave or in a bowl over a pan of simmering water.

Meanwhile, crumble the biscuits until you have large crumbs, then finely chop the crystallised orange or candied peel. Mix in a bowl then add the melted chocolate and stir together carefully.

Cover a plate or baking tray with greaseproof paper then, using a teaspoon, put dollops of the mixture on to the tray (make sure they are small enough to fit in your glasses). Leave to set in the fridge.

Put a crunchy chocolate ball in each glass. Stir the chocolate orange cream to make it slightly looser and easier to handle. With a piping bag or teaspoon, fill the glasses with a layer of cream. Keep in the fridge.

Just before serving, add the remaining crunchy chocolate balls and decorate with the candied orange and/or melted chocolate.

Sangria and chocolate

Preparation time: 25–30 minutes
+ 1 hour 30 minutes chilling
Cooking time: 10 minutes
Makes 8–12 desserts

Chocolate ganache with wine

1 orange
1 lemon
750 ml (26½ fl oz) red wine
2 cinnamon sticks
50 g (1¾ oz) icing sugar
500 g (1 lb 1½ oz) dark chocolate
(minimum 55% cocoa solids),
broken into small pieces

Sangria jelly

1 orange
3 sheets of gelatine
250 ml (8¾ fl oz) red wine
50 g (1¾ oz) icing sugar
1 green apple, cored and cut into
small pieces
125 g (4½ oz) redcurrants

To make the ganache, wash the orange and lemon, then cut into large pieces. Heat over a medium heat with the wine, cinnamon and sugar. Leave to simmer for 6–7 minutes.

Place the chocolate in a bowl and strain the warm wine over. Mix well. Fill your serving glasses two-thirds full with the ganache.

To make the jelly, peel the orange with a small knife then segment it, being careful to preserve the juice and peelings. Soften the gelatine in cold water.

Over a medium heat, heat the wine, sugar, orange juice and orange peelings. Simmer for 2–3 minutes.

Strain the hot mixture and dissolve the gelatine in it. Leave to cool at room temperature.

Cut the orange segments into small pieces and share between the well-chilled desserts, followed by the apple pieces and redcurrants.

Once the sangria jelly has cooled, pour over the desserts and leave to set in the fridge.

Chocolate meringue with apple

Preparation time. 45 minutes +
1 hour chilling
Cooking time: 15 minutes
Makes 6–8 desserts

1 kg (2 lb 3 oz) apples, peeled,
cored and chopped into small
pieces
15 sponge fingers

Apple jelly
7 sheets of gelatine
500 ml (17½ fl oz) good quality
apple juice
125 g (4½ oz) caster sugar

Chocolate mousse
150 g (5¼ oz) chocolate, broken into
pieces
1 dessertspoon Calvados
4 eggs, separated

Meringue
4 egg whites
100 g (3½ oz) caster sugar

To make the apply jelly, soften the
gelatine in cold water. Heat the apple
juice with the sugar until it boils.
Remove from the heat and add the
gelatine. Stir until it has dissolved.
Pour around 2 cm (¾ inch) of jelly
into the bottom of each serving glass.
Keep in the fridge.

Cook the apple pieces in the
microwave, little by little, on a plate
covered with cling film, or cook them
in a saucepan with a little water for a
few minutes until they soften slightly.
Divide in half and leave in the fridge.

For the chocolate mousse, gently
melt the chocolate in the microwave
or in a bowl over a pan of simmering
water. Add the calvados then the egg
yolks, one by one. Whisk the egg
whites into stiff peaks and gently fold
into the chocolate mixture.

Crumble the sponge fingers, sprinkle
into the glasses then add half the
apples. With a piping bag, fill the
glasses with chocolate mousse,
leaving 1–2 cm (½–¾ inch) at the
top. Return to the fridge.

For the meringue, whisk the egg
whites into stiff peaks, add the sugar
and whisk for another 1–2 minutes.
Stir in the rest of the apples. Use to
fill the glasses to the top and smooth
the surface.

Caramelise the surface with a blow
torch.

Just before serving, you can, if you
wish, heat the bottom of the desserts
in hot water to lightly liquify the jelly.

Chicory and chocolate parfait with salted caramel

Preparation time: 40 minutes +
3 hours freezing
Cooking time: 20 minutes
Makes 8–10 desserts

You will need a sugar thermometer,
a 500 ml (17½ fl oz) siphon with
gas cylinder and an electric whisk

Iced parfait
150 g (5¼ oz) icing sugar
70 ml (2½ fl oz) water
8 egg yolks
20 g (¾ oz) liquid or powdered
chicory extract
40 g (1½ oz) cocoa powder
500 ml (17½ fl oz) whipping cream

Caramel with salted butter
100 g (3½ oz) icing sugar
50 ml (1¾ fl oz) water
150 ml (5¼ fl oz) whipping cream
40 g (1½ oz) salted butter
2 pinches of sea salt

To make the parfait, bring the sugar and water to the boil and leave until they reach 120°C (250°F).

Beat the egg yolks using an electric whisk on a medium speed. Once the syrup has reached 120°C (250°F), pour into the egg yolks, little by little, increasing the speed of the mixer a bit. When the mix has doubled in volume, decrease the speed, add the chicory extract and cocoa powder and continue to beat until the mixture has cooled a little.

Meanwhile, pour the chilled cream into a bowl, place in a larger ice-filled container and whip. It should thicken until it sticks to the whisk but not become too firm. Very gently fold in the chicory and cocoa mixture.

Add to your serving glasses so that they are two-thirds full and put in the freezer for at least 3 hours.

For the caramel, heat the sugar and water over a medium heat until it reaches 170°C (340°F).

Meanwhile, heat the cream in the microwave until it is just beginning to boil.

Once the sugar has reached 170°C (340°F), remove the saucepan from the heat and add the cream (watch out for splashes), butter and salt then return to the heat, stirring constantly for 2–3 minutes. Leave to cool at room temperature.

Take the glasses out of the freezer and spoon two-thirds of the caramel on top of the parfait.

Put the remaining caramel in the siphon, screw on the gas cylinder and shake well. Siphon on the remaining caramel then serve straight away.

Tip: If you can't find liquid or powdered chicory use Camp chicory and coffee essence instead.

Iced cocoa nougat

Preparation time. 30–35 minutes
 + 3 hours freezing
Cooking time: 15 minutes
Makes 8–12 desserts

You will need a sugar thermometer
 and an electric whisk

150 g (5¼ oz) candied fruit
50 ml (1¾ fl oz) orange liqueur
180 g (6¼ oz) nuts (e.g. pistachios,
 almonds, hazelnuts)
180 g (6¼ oz) icing sugar
100 g (3½ oz) honey
50 g (1¾ oz) glucose
125 ml (4½ fl oz) water
500 ml (17½ fl oz) whipping cream
80 g (2¾ oz) cocoa powder
5 egg whites

In a bowl, soak the candied fruit in
the liqueur. Set aside.

Place the nuts and 100 g (3½ oz) of
sugar in a saucepan over a medium
heat. Heat and stir until caramelised.
Set aside.

In another saucepan, heat the honey,
glucose, water and 50 g (1¾ oz) of
sugar and leave until they reach
120°C (250°F).

Meanwhile, whip the well-chilled
cream. Add the cocoa powder and
keep in the fridge.

Whisk the egg whites into stiff peaks
with the electric mixer then add the
remaining 30 g (1 oz) of sugar and
beat again to firm up the egg whites.
Still beating at a lower speed, slowly
pour in the honey syrup and keep
beating until the meringue has
cooled.

Gently fold the caramelised nuts and
the candied fruit into the meringue
mixture then add the whipped
chocolate cream.

Pour the mixture into your serving
glasses, smooth the tops with a
spatula and put in the fridge for at
least 3 hours.

Iced lavender truffles

Preparation time: 15 minutes +
2 hours 30 minutes freezing
Cooking time: 6–7 minutes
Makes 6–8 desserts

You will need medium-sized,
dome-shaped silicone moulds
(if you want your desserts to
resemble the photograph) and
round-bottomed glasses

250 ml (8¾ fl oz) milk
5 g (¼ oz) lavender flowers
350 g (12¼ oz) milk chocolate,
broken into small pieces
200 g (7 oz) dark chocolate, broken
into small pieces
50 g (1¾ oz) unsalted butter, cut
into cubes
cocoa powder, for dusting

Heat the milk over a medium heat.
Once it starts to simmer, remove
from the heat and add the lavender
flowers. Leave to infuse away from
the heat for 2–3 minutes.

Place both chocolates and the butter
in a bowl. With a fine sieve, strain the
milk over the chocolates and butter.
Mix well until smooth.

Fill your serving glasses halfway with
half the chocolate cream and put the
other half in dome-shaped moulds.
Put everything in the freezer for
2 hours 30 minutes.

A few minutes before serving, turn
out the moulds and add the chocolate
domes to the glasses.

Dust with cocoa powder.

Tip: You can decorate the truffles
with lavender flowers if you wish.

Chocolate and Baileys granita

Preparation time: 10 minutes +
 3 hours freezing
Cooking time: 7 minutes
Makes 6–8 desserts

500 ml (17½ fl oz) water
100 g (3½ oz) icing sugar
3 dessertspoons cocoa powder
150 ml (5¼ fl oz) Baileys liqueur

In a saucepan, bring the water and sugar to the boil. Remove from the heat and add the cocoa powder. Mix well to blend in the cocoa.

Pour the syrup into a shallow bowl, leave to cool at room temperature then place in the freezer for 3 hours, mixing with a fork or whisk every 30 minutes to break up the ice crystals that will form.

Place your serving glasses in the freezer 30 minutes before serving.

Just before serving, fill the glasses with the chocolate granita and add a dash of Baileys to each.

Nine ways to serve chocolate ice cream

Sugary treats and sweets, for nostalgic childhood desserts...

Dried fruit, candied orange peel, pine nuts...

Fresh fruit adorned with a swirl of whipped cream or a baby meringue...

And every other single combination you can imagine to complement your chocolate ice cream! It's up to you to improvise.

1 **Bounty bar and a Morello cherry.**

2 **Iced lassi (add drinking yogurt).**

3 **Three oranges (candied orange peel, fresh orange and marmalade).**

4 **After Eight and fresh mint.**

5 **Gingerbread and dried apricots.**

6 **Chestnuts in syrup or candied chestnuts and toasted pine nuts.**

7 **Cherries with whipped cream and cherry coulis.**

8 **Sugared rose petals.**

9 **Meringue and summer berries of your choice.**

Banana brownies with vanilla rum cream

Preparation time: 25 minutes +
  1 hour 30 minutes chilling
Cooking time: 15 minutes
Makes 8–10 pairs of desserts

80 g (2¾ oz) icing sugar
4 bananas, sliced
400 g (14 oz) chocolate brownies,
  cut into small cubes

Vanilla and rum cream
250 ml (8¾ fl oz) milk
250 ml (8¾ fl oz) whipping cream
½ vanilla pod
6 egg yolks
90 g (3¼ oz) icing sugar
70 ml (2½ fl oz) dark rum

For the vanilla and rum cream, heat the milk, cream and seeds from the vanilla pod over a medium heat.

In a bowl, beat the egg yolks and sugar until the mixture turns pale.

Pour the boiling cream over the beaten eggs, mix well and return to a low heat in a saucepan. Mix constantly until the cream thickens and covers the back of the spoon. Make sure the cream does not boil.

Remove from the heat, add the rum then cover and place in the fridge.

In a frying pan, heat the sugar over a medium heat. Once it starts to caramelise, sauté the bananas for 1–2 minutes. Set aside 8–10 slices to decorate the desserts.

Mix the remaining bananas with the brownie cubes while still warm. Put in the fridge.

With a teaspoon, fill half your serving glasses with the banana and brownie mix and finish with a slice of caramelised banana. Fill the remaining glasses with the vanilla and rum cream. Eat well chilled.

Chilli–chocolate desserts with warm raspberry milk

Preparation time: 20 minutes +
 1 hour chilling
Cooking time: 10 minutes
Makes 4–6 desserts

100 g (3½ oz) fresh raspberries

Chilli and chocolate ganache
250 ml (8¾ fl oz) whipping cream
1 teaspoon chilli powder
250 g (8¾ oz) dark chocolate
 (minimum 58–70% cocoa solids),
 broken into small pieces
80 g (2¾ oz) butter, cut into cubes

Raspberry milk
750 ml (26 fl oz) milk
75 g (2½ oz) raspberry jam

To make the ganache, bring the cream and chilli powder to the boil in a saucepan over a medium heat. Place the chocolate and butter in a bowl and pour over the chilli cream. Mix well until smooth. Fill your serving glasses a third full and keep in the fridge for at least an hour.

Add a few raspberries to each glass once the ganache has set.

Just before serving, heat the milk and raspberry jam over a medium heat then pour into the glasses.

Pistachio and white chocolate milkshake with sour cherries

Preparation time: 10 minutes +
   1 hour chilling
Cooking time: 10 minutes
Makes 6–8 desserts

200 g (7 oz) frozen sour cherries
60 g (2 oz) icing sugar

**Pistachio and white chocolate
   milkshake**
2 scoops of white chocolate ice
   cream
4 scoops of pistachio ice cream
300 ml (10½ fl oz) milk
70 g (2½ oz) dark chocolate chips

Cook the cherries and sugar over a low heat, stirring occasionally, for 8–10 minutes. Keep in the fridge.

Put both ice creams, the milk and half the chocolate chips in a blender and blend for around 1 minute.

Add a layer of cooked cherries to the bottom of each serving glass and then fill with the milkshake.

Decorate with a sprinkle of chocolate chips and serve immediately.

Index

Conversion tables

The tables below are only approximate and are meant to be used as a guide only.

Approximate American/ European conversions

	USA	Metric	Imperial
brown sugar	1 cup	170 g	6 oz
butter	1 stick	115 g	4 oz
butter/ margarine/ lard	1 cup	225 g	8 oz
caster and granulated sugar	2 level tablespoons	30 g	1 oz
caster and granulated sugar	1 cup	225 g	8 oz
currants	1 cup	140 g	5 oz
flour	1 cup	140 g	5 oz
golden syrup	1 cup	350 g	12 oz
ground almonds	1 cup	115 g	4 oz
sultanas/ raisins	1 cup	200 g	7 oz

Approximate American/ European conversions

American	European
1 teaspoon	1 teaspoon/ 5 ml
½ fl oz	1 tablespoon/ ½ fl oz/ 15 ml
¼ cup	4 tablespoons/ 2 fl oz/ 50 ml
½ cup plus 2 tablespoons	¼ pint/ 5 fl oz/ 150 ml
1¼ cups	½ pint/ 10 fl oz/ 300 ml
1 pint/ 16 fl oz	1 pint/ 20 fl oz/ 600 ml
2½ pints (5 cups)	1.2 litres/ 2 pints
10 pints	4.5 litres/ 8 pints

Liquid measures

Imperial	ml	fl oz
1 teaspoon	5	
2 tablespoons	30	
4 tablespoons	60	
¼ pint/ 1 gill	150	5
⅓ pint	200	7
½ pint	300	10
¾ pint	425	15
1 pint	600	20
1¾ pints	1000 (1 litre)	35

Oven temperatures

American	Celsius	Fahrenheit	Gas Mark
Cool	130	250	½
Very slow	140	275	1
Slow	150	300	2
Moderate	160	320	3
Moderate	180	350	4
Moderately hot	190	375	5
Fairly hot	200	400	6
Hot	220	425	7
Very hot	230	450	8
Extremely hot	240	475	9

Other useful measurements

Measurement	Metric	Imperial
1 American cup	225 ml	8 fl oz
1 egg, size 3	50 ml	2 fl oz
1 egg white	30 ml	1 fl oz
1 rounded tablespoon flour	30 g	1 oz
1 rounded tablespoon cornflour	30 g	1 oz
1 rounded tablespoon caster sugar	30 g	1 oz
2 level teaspoons gelatine	10 g	¼ oz